Preparation while you wait

REAL TALK FOR WOMEN OF GOD
WAITNG ON THEIR PROMISE

KEISA JONES

Preparation While You Wait
Real Talk (Testimony), Tips & Scriptures for
Celibate Women of God Waiting on their Promise
Copyright © 2018 **Keisa Jones**

Published by Exodus Christian Publishing
www.ExodusChristianPublishing.com

Unless otherwise noted, all scriptures are from the KING JAMES VERSION (KJV): KING JAMES VERSION, public domain.

Scriptures marked (AMP) are taken from the AMPLIFIED BIBLE (AMP): Scripture taken from the AMPLIFIED® BIBLE, Copyright © 1954, 1958, 1962, 1964, 1965, 1987 by the Lockman Foundation Used by Permission. (www.Lockman.org)

Scripture quotations marked (NIV) are taken from the Holy Bible, New International Version®, NIV®. Copyright © 1973, 1978, 1984, 2011 by Biblica, Inc.™ Used by permission of Zondervan. All rights reserved worldwide. www.zondervan.com The "NIV" and "New International Version" are trademarks registered in the United States Patent and Trademark Office by Biblica, Inc.™

ISBN: 9781730945038

Book cover design by Kristine Cotterman - Exodus Design Studio
www.ExodusDesign.com

First printing: 2018

Printed in the United States of America

Contact
For Booking and other Events, Prophetess Keisa Jones can be reached:
By Phone: (442) 600-4191
By Email: Keisajones32@gmail.com or PreparationWhileYouWait@gmail.com

Dedication & Acknowledgements

First and foremost, this book is dedicated to my Lord and Savior Jesus Christ. Everything I am and will be is a result of the loving kindness He has shown me. Who would have thought Keisa Jones would ever be in a place or position to write a book; He did! Only His miraculous healing and deliverance could have catapulted me into a place of being ready to receive the promised husband.

Secondly, I would like to thank Prophetess Fannette Douglas for speaking and stirring up the gift of God contained within my heart. It is because of your push, accountability and challenge to write it out; have I completed what God purposed me to do. I am so grateful for your commitment to the Father and the wisdom He has given you to share with others.

To My Spiritual Parents Bishop Larnie and Elder Helen White; thank you for imparting so much wisdom, knowledge, and faith into my spirit. From the beginning, you have supported and pushed me to be the woman of God I am today. From the late nights at the church to the phone conversations; you have been there. Thank you for your prayers.

To my children, Kentaivia, Jeremiah and granddaughter Olivia; thank you for your patience. There were many times I was too tired to do anything, and you would let me off the hook and help me any way you could. I love each of you with all of my heart.

Lastly, I dedicate this book to the women who desire to be pure and holy before the Father. It is my desire that the words contained in this book challenge you to press and persevere beyond your flesh to the place of wholeness and expectation.

Table of Contents

Foreword
by Bishop Larnie J. White

"*Preparation While You Wait*" is an opportunity to take a close up and personal look at the author (Keisa Jones) personal testimony. She is very open and transparent about her journey from a life of promiscuity to a life that is totally and completely devoted and dedicated to God. This book is a must read for every young single woman and man. In a time when most folk's attitude towards dating, premarital sex, and all intimate relationships are so carefree and extremely casual, it's refreshing to know that there is still someone who have good, moral, biblical principles. We are so proud of the author, Keisa Jones, who is our spiritual daughter, for her love for God and His Word. She has remained loyal, faithful and totally committed to her personal relationship with God for 10 years. I know this because my wife and I served as her Spiritual Covering for 8 of those 10 years. This book is a very easy read and power packed with very practical information and should be shared with every single person you know and come in contact with. God bless you Keisa, and I know that we are going to be hearing more from you soon.

Foreword
by Dr. Helen Delores White

My dearest daughter, Evangelist, and Prophetess, Keisa Monique Jones, you are greatly loved and chosen of God. Our hearts will forever be intertwined by the golden threads of love from our father.

It is with Jesus joy and humble esteem I pen my thoughts and endorsement of this beautiful testimony given by you in your book inspired by the Holy Spirit. Truly you are the one to tell your story and impact the lives of countless people who will read, share and chose to do it God's way.

"Preparation While You Wait" is a powerful message. You passed the test. It is no small matter to spend "ten" years preparing for one of the most incredible assignments a woman can accept from God. That is the first step in a life changed forever, the life of a wife. The biblical meaning of the number ten is the completed course of time or completeness in divine order. Ten is used to describe anything that is near to perfection. It is the symbol of matter in harmony. Ten also represents the creator and the creation. So, as I look closely at ten, I realize that God's purpose is perfected through your obedience. It had to be this way!

According to scripture, a wife found is a "Good thing" and, of course, she must be found. Therefore, your husband will put much effort, diligence, and patience in the search for you. He is looking, and you will not be easily found. Why, because you have been shrouded with the "Word" and a covering of "Faith." May I add, the book has only begun. There will be other books in a series until the entire story is told.

It took only twelve months for Esther (the Jewish maiden for the Queen) to prepare to meet the King. Esther also had the best help for her time of purification. On the other hand, Ruth, the Moabites, was married to a Jew for "ten" years. Her only preparation for "Boaz" was faith in her mother-in-law's God, and her willingness to follow Naomi's instructions. I draw from these parallels that the time of preparation for your "Boaz" seems to be that in comparison to Naomi and Ruth. Trust and obey.

Why you had to wait is not the question because we know that the plan of God cannot be rushed, manipulated, recreated or prevented; when and where will be answered soon. As you acknowledged, God knew you before you were formed in your mother's womb. Therefore, He knew that your testimony of the time of preparation would bring the greatest glory!

I'm so thankful to have been chosen to walk with you from the beginning. Thankful that God gave me the spirit of a "fireman" because I had to talk you down from many trees you climbed in an attempt jump down and abort the assignment of *"Preparation While You Wait."*

May this story be told for countless generations of women and men who will trust the process of *"Preparation While You Wait."*

Foreword
by Fannette Douglas

Keisa Jones, (a single mother) is a truly prophetic voice that God has raised up in this season to proclaim the heart of God and to touch lives from all walks of life especially women who are struggling to remain pure before almighty God. Her life and ministry are characterized by humility, love, integrity, truth, commitment, and compassion. She is bold but yet humble and has a clear understanding of her mantle.

While writing her book, I had the pleasure to read each chapter of *"Preparation While you Wait."* I can honestly say that her book is packed with wisdom and instructions on how to stand in times of Temptations. Keisa gives readers the testimony of her triumphs and failures; her fantasies and realities; her fears and expectations; her healing and her deliverance. She is transparent about her truths. One of my favorites is Chapter 10, DATING GOD, where she learns to be intimate (have fellowship) with God and in doing so, falls in love with Him all over again.

This book was written to help single ladies who are struggling to stay celibate and no longer desire to give their bodies to every man they date. *"Preparation While You Wait"* is a must-have in every single woman's library. It will help you in your effort to stay Celibate/Pure while you wait for who God has for you. I encourage you to read the book, follow the instructions and watch your life SHIFT!

Lastly, Bishop Douglas and I are proud of Keisa. It is an honor to serve in the Kingdom of God with her and witness God's next move in her life.

Introduction

Why is it taking so long God? Where is he? Have I missed him? What have I done? Are there any saved men still available? Will I be alone for the rest of my life? I found myself asking these questions after my first year of celibacy. It was such a struggle! I was no stranger to intimacy (sex) and understood this would be one of the greatest fights of my life; fighting to honor my promise to the Lord. I was determined to honor God and preserve my body unto Him. He tells us in His word, *"Do you not know that your body is a temple of the Holy Spirit who is within you, whom you have [received as a gift] from God, and that you are not your own [property]?" (1 Corinthians 6:19 AMP)* I understood I did not belong to myself; I had been purchased for a price, *"For you are bought with a price: therefore glorify God in your body, and in your spirit, which are God's" (1 Corinthians 6:20 KJV).*

I wanted for the first time in my life to Glorify God with my body, but there was a battle going on in my members. I was going through withdrawal! I wanted to have sex, but I knew I wanted God more than momentary sexual gratification. To accomplish this (through faith) I understood I needed to shut down my phone and turn off the television. Everything was a temptation. People I hadn't heard from in years, called. People I hadn't come in contact with, all of a sudden appeared in the grocery store, at the bank and school. I even had someone pop up at my job professing their love for me!

Scripture tells us in I Corinthians 10:13, *"No temptation [regardless of its source] has overtaken or enticed you that is not common to human experience [nor is any temptation unusual or beyond human resistance]; but God is faithful [to His word—He is compassionate and trustworthy], and He will not let you be tempted beyond your ability [to resist], but along with the temptation He [has in the past and is now and] will [always] provide* **the way** *out as well, so that you will be able to endure it [without yielding, and will overcome temptation with joy]"*. What a relief knowing I was not alone and that He has already provided THE WAY to escape. So, I waited!

As the days began to progress and the days turned into years, I let doubt creep in. Is this it for me? I began to think on all the times I fornicated; all the times I lay with someone who did not value me. All the times I gave myself away. I thought about all the times I sinned against my own body. I found myself crying out to God and the process of healing and forgiving me began. I knew God forgave me, but I needed to release myself from the guilt, hurt and shame. I went to bed that night, and God gave me a brief glimpse of him; the one He saved for me.

Each year I began to declare, "This is my year." I started looking up wedding dresses. I lived on Pinterest. I watched, *"Say Yes to the Dress"* religiously. I picked out the décor and flower arrangements. My Bridesmaids will wear this, and my daughter will wear that. I had it all together but no husband. By the end of the year (December) I was hurt and confused but then the New Year (January) would come around, and the process repeated itself. I declared, "This is my year!" However, I saw no husband in sight. As a matter of fact, no one and I do mean NOT ONE man would ask for my number (lol). I didn't even get asked out on a date. It was as if I was in a bubble and no one could see me. I felt separated from reality. I remember lying on my bed one morning asking God why me. It was in that moment I heard the voice of the Lord say, "To whom much is given, much is required. Great is the sacrifice Keisa". I knew God had assigned a specific man for me, so dating wasn't an option. Why did I need someone specific? Why did I have to wait longer than everyone else? Just let me meet him I cried. Still, I waited.

It wasn't until after the fifth year the Lord finally responded to my questions from the first year. I heard Him say, "He (your husband) is waiting for you to get yourself together Keisa." Wow! This was a tough pill to swallow. I thought I was ready. I thought I had it together. Waiting for me? This can't be true. The spirit of pride (a feeling or deep pleasure or satisfaction derived from one's own achievements, the achievements of those with whom one is closely associated, or from qualities or possessions that are widely admired) will prevent you from seeing the real condition of your heart.

For the next few years, I found myself struggling with the idea of not being ready. I began to rebel against the very words God spoke to me. I started listening to R & B love songs which opened the door for the spirit of loneliness to consume me. I wrestled with anger as those around me where getting married. This sent me into moments of depression and sadness. I spent days ignoring God's holy conviction; ignoring the voice of the Lord; moving further and further from His presence.

What a waste of time this was! God is faithful to His word and does not make special arrangements and does not change His word because we don't receive it. I remember hearing the Holy Spirit say, "God is not moved by your emotions Keisa, but by your faith in Him and His plan for your life." I finally got to the place where I needed to be all along; in His word. I turned to the scriptures and found my strength and my help. Scriptures like *Isaiah 41:10, "Do not fear, for I am with you; do not anxiously look about you, for I am your God I will strengthen you, surely I will help you, surely I will uphold you with My righteous right hand."* I found comfort in scriptures like that of Deuteronomy 31:8 which says, *"The LORD is the one who goes ahead of you; He will be with you, He will not fail you or forsake you. Do not fear or be dismayed.* Oh, what strength I received when I read Isaiah 43:2, *"When you pass through the waters, I will be with you; And through the rivers, they will not overflow you; when you walk through the fire, you will not be scorched, nor will the flame burn you."*

After year eight I finally submitted to God's plan and His word. As soon as I submitted, He began to pour into me, and for the first time, I was ready to receive. I wanted to go through the PROCESS of being

PROCESSED. I wanted to be in a position where I could receive the man He (God) prepared for me and not run him (my husband) away.

As I walk into my tenth year of celibacy, my hope is that this book acknowledges the struggle (REAL TALK and TESTIMONY) women of God encounter while walking pure before the Lord yet confirming God's word, "W*e can do all things through Christ Who strengthens us (Philippians 4:13).* My desire is that the wisdom (7 TIPS) found in this book challenges and encourages those waiting faithfully to use this time to do a self-check-up in preparation for His Promise. Finally, my purpose of writing this book is for the Word of God (SCRIPTURES) to strengthen and catapult you into a place of expectation with thanksgiving knowing that He who has promised is faithful (Hebrews 10:23).

Chapter 1

The Call (My Testimony)

The last night I slept with him would be the start of God delivering me from the Strong Man of fornication and all the demonic spirits attached to it. I had no idea that in a few weeks my life would change so drastically! This is my testimony, and I share it to glorify God. I share it in detail so you can understand the magnitude of His delivering power and so you will know I am **well qualified** to speak on this matter! The ability to be in a place of preparation I take no credit for. It is by the delivering power of Jesus and His word that I am here today!

It was a month before my 30th birthday, and I was tired and worn out. I had recently discovered I was being cheated on. This was not the first time this happened to me but for some reason this time was different. Very quickly I went from being upset about being cheated on (by an individual I gave over 10 years of my life to) to accepting a position as the other woman in what I call a "demonic love triangle." It was so draining! I was going back and forth on this emotional ride, and it felt like the worst rollercoaster experience ever. I stayed sick and not wanting to eat. I was so hurt and crushed but I convinced myself some time with him was better than no time with him. I mean I had given 10 years to him and didn't want to let it end. Who would want me after two kids? I was so discouraged and defeated. I didn't want to start over, so I settled.

It was two in the morning, and he promised he would stay the night with me. He received a phone call from the other woman and said he needed to leave. He owed me some money, so he left it on my pillow. I remember lying in bed after he left feeling less than a woman. I felt I was a prostitute. I knew I deserved better. I knew there was much more for me. I knew, at that moment, I had a greater purpose in life. I knew deep down inside there was a greater plan for me and it did not include this. *(For I know the plans and thoughts that I have for you,' says the Lord, 'plans for peace and well-being and not for disaster, to give you a future and a hope. (Jeremiah 29:11 AMP)*

A few days later I found myself sitting in my living room on the couch angry and upset. He had promised again to spend time with me. He said he would come over and spend time with me. He never showed up. He made up an excuse, but he knew it would be okay with me; that I would not hold him accountable. He knew I would accept it because I did the week before. I allowed this cycle to repeat itself weekly (Now that I look back I see it was a divine set up for my deliverance).

I flipped through the channels of the television and I came upon a video playing by Kirk Franklin. There was a young lady who was in bed looking at a man as he got dressed and walked away. It appeared they had just finished having sex and now he was preparing to leave. The look of shame on her face and sadness I knew all too well. I remember looking at this video and saying, "Is this me?" Just a few days prior this was my exact storyline. As I continued to watch "*Imagine Me*," I listened to the words and began to cry. I cried as I saw myself in this young lady, but I couldn't imagine myself being free. Scripture says in the book of Galatians, we were called to be free, but I was trapped and lost. I wanted to imagine being in this place of freedom. At the very end of the video, as this young lady sat on the bed, Kirk Franklin comes in (portraying God) and whispers something in her ear. She smiles and gets up dancing. What kind of liberty is this? I remembered thinking. I recall her so happy and singing that it's gone. It's not that simple I yelled, and I turned the television off.

I received a phone call from another man (who I would occasionally have sex with) and invited him over to spend some time with me. When you are lost in fornication and longing for love, you are willing to accept it from anywhere and anyone. We went out to eat and came back to my home. While walking to my bedroom, I felt uneasy. I can't explain it in words, but I knew it was wrong. It was like a spiritual alarm went off in my spirit. This is the first time I felt this way. As I continued to the act of fornicating (having sex), I heard *A VOICE* say to me, "What you are doing is filthy and nasty!" Who was this? I remember thinking to myself. I looked up at the man I was with, and he had heard nothing. I said to myself; I must be going crazy and ignored *THE VOICE*.

The following night I got a call from the one I really wanted to be with. The one I was trapped in a demonic love triangle with asking to see me. He said he wanted to spend some time with me, so I agreed. We walked to my bedroom, and I remember feeling the exact same way I did the night before; uneasy. While in the act of fornication (having sex) again I heard *THE VOICE* speak again. It was so clear but much louder than the night before. "I said what you are doing is filthy and nasty!" I looked around again and didn't see anything, but in my heart, I knew it was God. I was not raised in the church and had no idea who Jesus was, but I recognized this was *THE ONE* who created me and knew me before I was formed in my mother's womb. He was calling out to me! He had come to save me!

I was eager for him (my boyfriend) to leave. I wanted to commune with *THE ONE* who was calling out to me. After he left, I got on my knees and cried out to *THE VOICE* who was calling me. I repented and asked Him to forgive me. I told Him I had tried to stop before, but I couldn't. I told Him I was addicted to sex, pornography, and masturbation. I told Him all of my secrets; things I had never shared with anyone. I was naked (open and truthful) before Him. I asked Him to please forgive me and help me! I wept so much that my carpet was saturated with tears. I wanted His help! I didn't know who He was, but I knew He was real. I was unwilling to continue in my sin, depression, and anger. The overwhelming desire to be free was a priority at this moment. I thought to myself since He is here, I will not hold back anything. I pleaded with Him to cleanse me and make me whole. I cried, "Take it away!" Take away the guilt, shame, embarrassment, hurt and pain! *"Come to Me, all who are weary and heavily burdened [by religious rituals that provide no peace], and I will give you rest [refreshing your souls with salvation]. Take My yoke upon you and learn from Me [following Me as My disciple], for I am gentle and humble in heart, and you will find rest (renewal, blessed quiet) for your souls. For My yoke is easy [to bear] and My burden is light." (Matthew 11:28-30)*

I finally got up from the floor drenched in tears. I thought I was crying for a few minutes but had actually poured out before the Lord between 4-5 hours. It was now the morning. Where did the time go? I looked around my room, and it was so bright. Is this my room? It was so clean and fresh. I realized, at that moment, God had done everything I asked Him to do. When I cried out to Him; He answered me immediately! *"In my distress I called to the LORD; I cried to my God for help. From His temple He heard my voice; my cry came before Him, into His ears" (Psalm 18:6 NIV).*

The bedroom I had used to sin against God with my body, had been washed and purified by His grace, mercy, and love. I heard the birds singing outside my window. The sun was shining so brightly. It was like I was born all over again; given a fresh start! *"Remember ye not the former things, neither consider the things of old. Behold, I will do a new thing; now it shall spring forth; shall ye not know it? I will even make a way in the wilderness, and rivers in the desert. The beast of the field shall honour Me, the dragons and the owls: because I give waters in the wilderness, and rivers in the desert, to give drink to My people, My chosen. This people have I formed for Myself; they shall shew forth My praise" (Isaiah 43:18-21 KJV).*

I walked over to my dresser to take my daily birth control pill, and I heard **THE VOICE OF GOD** speak. He said I no longer needed the pill since I had given my life over to Him. He reminded me of my promise and told me to trust Him. I said yes Lord and grabbed all the pills (a 6-month supply) and flushed them down the toilet. I felt as if 10,000 weights had been lifted from me. I was free! I had received the spirit of liberation! I realized, at that moment, I had a supernatural experience with my King, and He said I was His princess. I remember having a smile on my face. *"Now the Lord is that Spirit: and where the Spirit of the Lord [is], there [is] liberty" (2 Corinthians 3:17 KJV).* It was all gone like the young lady in the video sang! I was now singing that song! I was now experiencing the joy she portrayed in the video. It was true! Hallelujah!

Chapter Two

Warring with the Flesh

Oxford Living Dictionary describes war as a state of armed conflict between different countries or different groups within a country. In my case, I was warring now between my spirit and flesh. My spirit was now reconnected to God, but my flesh was in total opposition! There were two natures within me battling against each other. The battle was not just on the outside but inside as well. Paul said it this way, *"For I joyfully delight in the law of God in my inner self [with my new nature], but I see a different law and rule of action in the members of my body [in its appetites and desires], waging war against the law of my mind and subduing me and making me a prisoner of the law of sin which is within my members"* *(Romans 7:22-23 AMP).*

I loved God, but I wanted to have sex! Every time I turned on the television, there was sex. When I listened to the radio, everyone was talking about sex. When I was having sex, I do not recall all of these conversations regarding it (lol). There is a saying I've heard and discovered its truth, "You never miss what you never had." Well, I had it, and I wanted it desperately! I was getting phone calls from people I never mentioned I liked; all of a sudden, they liked me. While driving my car, I was being flagged down and told how beautiful I was. I remember one day it was so hard. I left work and sat on the couch and turned the television on.

There was a song by Trey Songz playing, and it was called *"SEX."* I had someone stop at my home, and after using the restroom, he came out with his pants down. I fled! I literally had to ban this individual from my home. I could not make this up if I wanted to!

The Lord began to speak to me concerning what was happening. He said I was under spiritual attack and this would be a time of testing for me. He said I was an overcomer now and could do all things through Him because He had strengthened me. I heard His words, but I did not enjoy this battle. I felt like I was in the ring with Mike Tyson getting beat down and it was only the 1st round with 11 more to go. I found my body reacting to things I did not give it permission to. I would have sexually perverted dreams so demonic, I can't even share; *"Wretched and miserable man that I am! Who will [rescue me and] set me free from this body of death [this corrupt, mortal existence]? Thanks be to God [for my deliverance] through Jesus Christ our Lord! (Romans 7:24-27 AMP)*

The flesh is an enemy to God. Scripture tells us in Romans 8:17 *a mind set on the flesh is hostile toward God; for it does not subject itself to the law of God, for it is not even able to do so.* There is no way to fight this battle successfully in the flesh. It's impossible. The only way to kill the flesh is to submit to Gods word; *"So submit to [the authority of] God. Resist the devil [stand firm against him], and he will flee from you"* (James 4:7 AMP). I made a decision that I would shut all forms of communication down. No more visitors to my home. I turned my phone off along with the television. When I got home from work, I would cook for my children and then lock myself in my bedroom praying and crying out to God. I listened to music that only glorified God. I watched television shows which proclaimed the Good News of Jesus Christ.

When the enemy found I was no longer enticed by sex, he found another area to attack me; fear. Supernatural disturbances would keep me up all night long. At one point I can remember being up for 72 hours afraid to go to sleep. I didn't know what was happening. I thought maybe this is God. Maybe He is trying to get my attention. Then I read in His word He has not given me the spirit of fear but one of power, love and a sound mind. I discovered I needed more power to defeat the attacks of this low-down dirty enemy. Satan does not play fair! His ultimate desire is to steal, kill and destroy! The enemy thought fear would be the catalyst to drive me back into the spirit of pervasion. Understand he will use anything to get you back under his grip!

My spirit needed to be strengthened by the Word of God. Listen; there is no way around it! I started to get stronger the more I read His Word. Things that bothered me were no longer upsetting me. Phone calls no longer had power over me. The Word of God is so POWERFUL; it's as sharp as a surgeon's scalpel, cutting through everything! Nothing can defend itself against the Word of God. There is no weapon greater and more dominant! The more I meditated on His Word, the more I wanted Him and less of sex. There is no way to walk upright before the Lord without His Spirit, His Power, and His Word.

The moment I understood the battle may have been formed but was already won by the BLOOD of Jesus; the sooner I flowed in His Power and Victory. There was no need to fight the battle from a defeated position. I was already declared a champion over my flesh because of His strength. I boldly stood on the scripture found in 1 John 4:4, *"Little children (believers, dear ones), you are of God and you belong to Him and have [already] overcome them [the agents of the antichrist]; because He who is in you is greater than he (Satan) who is in the world [of sinful mankind]"* Like David took out Goliath with 1 smooth stone; I found through the Word of God, I could slay this flesh and bring it under subjection by the power of the Holy Spirit. I knew I could not survive without the Holy Spirit.

Reflection

Take a moment and write down the area(s) you continue to struggle (war against) within the flesh. List them below. After composing the list, I challenge you to go the Scripture! The only way to OVERCOME it is through the Word of God. What does the Scriptures say? After writing down what the Scripture says, it's time to declare it (the Word) over your situation!

_____

_____

_____

_____

_____

_____

_____

_____

_____

_____

_____

_____

_____

_____

_____

Chapter Three

Overcoming Disappointments

Now that my flesh was under control, I waited patiently for my husband's arrival. I remember having a dream walking down the aisle of a church holding someone's hand. I couldn't see anything but his arm and hand. I thought to myself, "Wow I just got saved, and I'm getting married!" Six months in and God has moved! God is magnificent! As I journeyed down the aisle, I remember such an overwhelming peace. What a beautiful experience this was. My heart was overcome with excitement; tears flowed down my face. Then I woke up and began to thank God for my soon to come husband. I magnified His Name for my wait was over I declared!!!

Then He dropped the TRUTH on me. The Holy Spirit said the dream I had was not of a natural husband, but I was now wedded to Him. *"For your husband is your Maker, The Lord of hosts is His name; and your Redeemer is the Holy One of Israel, Who is called the God of the whole earth" (Isaiah 54:5 AMP).* Wow! Although I was excited about my new relationship with my Creator, I must admit I was a little disappointed.

Several years would pass, and I was still not married. I was so frustrated with God and the wait. One day while driving He asked me why I was so mad at Him. I told Him I was not angry. God knows all things, so I'm not sure why I didn't come clean. I mean He is The Alpha and

Omega! He told me I didn't say it verbally, but I was showing it by not reading His word and not talking with Him (praying). Thank God for Grace and Mercy! I began to tell Him I was hurt because everyone around me was either getting married or dating but I myself was lonely. God shared with me I was set apart for a specific man and could not date. He stated my marriage would be a divine connection for the advancement of His Kingdom. He stated it was much bigger than physical companionship, but it was about His Kingdom! This was heavy. I never looked at it from this perspective. Honestly, I really wanted to have sex (and God knew this), but I understood it was much deeper than the physical! I understood the weight of the divine covenant I made with the Father when I submitted myself to Him. When I said yes, I meant yes by any means necessary. However, I was still disappointed.

A few weeks later I went out of the state on a mini-vacation. I started engaging and developing a friendship (conversation) with a young man. I knew deep down in my heart I was not to be entangled with this friendship. I look back and know I was rebelling against God. I knew immediately He was not the one, but I continued the conversation. It felt good to have someone interested in me after many years of feeling like I was invisible. The flesh and your emotions can cause you to lose sight of the truth.

One night as I lay in my bed the Holy Spirit said very clearly to me, "Shut the conversation down." He said to cut it off; it was distracting and hindering me from His next divine move. I was so saddened. I didn't really want to be with the person, but I was in love with the idea of having someone from the opposite sex to communicate with. The following day I did as I was instructed; shutting down the friendship/dialogue. I cried out to God! I'm lonely! At this point, it was not about anything sexual but more about having someone to talk with. I wanted the conversation, but I needed God more. The Lord reminded me of the commitment I made to Him again. He reminded me of my call to sacrifice; *"From everyone to whom much has been given, much will be required; and to whom they entrusted much, of him they will ask all the more" (Luke 12:48 AMP).*

I had to let it go! I had to overcome the disappointment and sadness I felt. I was different! I was chosen! I needed to break the seed of disappointment that had taken root in my heart. The dismantling of the seed began when I got honest with God. When He asked me why I was angry with Him; I was not 100% honest. I had to lay it all out. When I did this, I felt the spirit of heaviness lift. At this moment I was willing to surrender my will over to His. I had to pray for my hearts desires to align with His perfect plan for me. I understood I needed Him to renew my mind and guide me. He alone knew the path I needed to take, *"For My thoughts are not your thoughts, nor are your ways My ways," declares the Lord. For as the heavens are higher than the earth, so are My ways higher than your ways and My thoughts higher than your thoughts" (Isaiah 55:8-9 AMP).*

Disappointments last only for a moment if we allow God's perfect plan for our lives to overrule without objecting! He alone knows our ending from the beginning and what's ultimately best for us. Scripture says that He is the Author and Finisher of our faith. He is THE ARCHITECT; and Designer. He alone constructs the blueprint design for our lives. I discovered my lack of understanding of God's will and plan for my life was the root of my disappointment. The frustration I felt was centered on the lack of accepting God's design. I learned God does not always reveal His plans! There are some things He keeps hidden because He knows we can't handle the revelation of it. When you don't understand or when you don't see, you must trust.

Many times, we believe no one understands or possibly we are the only one going through a particular situation. We are not the first and will not be the last of those who had to overcome disappointments. I am reminded of the story of Job in the Scriptures. He was a man who walked up right before the Lord and shunned all evil. In the span of literally one day, he lost everything! He lost his children, livestock, and servants. Talk about disappointment! Can you imagine the pain and disappointment Job experienced after this great loss? Later on, we find his wife turns against him as well as his friends. Job begins to question God and starts to compare life to darkness. After the pain and disappointment, we find God restores Job. Job receives a double portion, children, and livestock. He goes on to live a long life! Throughout the process, Job struggled to trust God and hold on to His word. Job was unaware of what the outcome would be, but God knew from the beginning. Like Job, we have suffered great disappointment in life. Through the process, we can't see the end results in its totality, but God always knows! Like Job; God will give us double for our trouble. He takes delight in blessing His children, but it's through our obedience to His will.

Reflection

There is a process of overcoming disappointment. Initially you are frustrated; sad. Frustration turns into a place of trying to understand why? Why is this happening? Why can't I just have it? Why must I wait? This place pushes you into a place of loneliness and depression. Then we finally get real and honest with God; submitting to His Will! This is the place He reveals His plans for our life. After reading this chapter on overcoming disappointments; what are some of the disappointments you have experienced? Why were you disappointed? What stage are you in your disappointment? Write it out.

_____

_____

_____

_____

_____

Chapter Four
Submitting to God

I discovered very quickly there is no way to overcome disappointment, hurt and frustration until there is a surrendering of the will. Doing this is never an easy thing. The flesh is never satisfied and craves to operate from a place of selfishness. Submitting is a necessary part of the process of aligning with God's perfect will for our lives. The definition of submit, according to Webster Dictionary, simply is to yield oneself to the authority or will of another. We understand the Higher Authority we yield to is God. He is the Final Authority!

There is no way to submit all our expectations in life to Him without first trusting Him! Trust is one of the keys which give us access to His thoughts regarding us. In trusting Him, we are able to release/die to self and receive more of Him. When we give ourselves away to the One who knew us before we were formed in our mother's womb; we are awakened to His plans for us; *"For I know the plans and thoughts that I have for you says the Lord; plans for peace and well-being and not for disaster, to give you a future and a hope" (Jeremiah 29:11 AMP).* When we do this; we have access to exceedingly more than we gave up and we will not be dissatisfied! Scripture tells us in Romans 10:11, *"Whoever believes in Him [whoever adheres to, trusts in, and relies on Him] will not be disappointed [in his expectations]" (AMP).* We will not be disappointed when it's all said and down! Humility is another key that gives us the ability and capacity to submit. It's a crucial piece of the puzzle. Realizing we are nothing and can do nothing without Him is an overwhelming yet remarkable revelation. There is no room for arrogance and pride! Pride is the opposite of humility, and they can't both operate in the same space. Scripture tells us God resists the proud and a proud look is one of the six things He hates. We have to make a choice daily to walk in humility and submit to God. When we walk in humility, we grow, develop and mature spiritually.

Trust, humility, and submission allowed me to see things from God's perspective. When I looked at my life through His lens (His viewpoint); I discovered I was a mess at best. I understood I was in no way, shape, form, or fashion, ready to take on the full responsibilities of a Godly wife. In submitting to Him, I learned I was broken and hurt. I was in no way equipped for the husband He prepared for me. I finally came into agreement with the word God shared a few years before; my husband was waiting for me to get myself together. In this place, I shifted my focus off of wanting a husband desperately to urgently wanting to be made whole. I was ready to be processed and cleansed from the inside out (deep cleansing). I wanted; better yet I needed deliverance and healing! I understood there could be no residue if I wanted to maintain a healthy marriage. If I was going to be ready to handle the weight of a marriage; the process of deliverance was not an option. I needed old thoughts and ideas to be shattered (destroyed) in order to be a partner in this Kingdom assignment!

I challenge you to get in a place of trusting the Lord, humbling yourself and submitting to His plan. In the posture of humility is where He will reveal to you His secrets and plans for your life. It's also in this place; you will be a willing participant in His desire to develop, cultivate and strengthen you!

Reflection

Scripture says, "Submit yourselves ,then, to God. Resist the devil, and he will flee from you." (James 4:7) In order for the enemy to flee from us (while trying to remain pure before the Lord) we must submit to God first! What has prevented you from submitting totally to God in this process? Write it down! Now go to the Scripture. What does the Word say? Declare what the Word says over it!

_____

_____

_____

_____

_____

_____

_____

_____

_____

_____

_____

_____

_____

_____

_____

Chapter Five

Preparation Tip 1:
Repent and Denounce Ungodly Soul Ties

When we submit to God and humble ourselves; the process of healing begins. This is when He (the Holy Spirit) shows us the condition of our hearts and gives us the strategies necessary to be delivered! While in the process (development phase); this is an opportunity to get ready for what God has promised (those who desire to be married). Failure to complete the process will result in the inability to handle the responsibility, challenges, and hardships connected to being married. Yes, I said it! Marriage will have some rough patches and difficult moments. Contrary to popular belief it's not perfect. Rushing through the process and/or not completing the process will lead to emotional choices outside the will of God. It can cause you to settle and miss out on the fullness of what God has prepared specifically for you! You could quite possibly ruin and or not truly appreciate the blessing of marriage. You can have what you want but can you handle what you get? I'm not going to charge you for that nugget!

A soul tie can be defined as a strong soul connection, bond, link, or yoke formed between two individuals either emotionally and/or physically. Soul ties can be positive or negative and can be formed in many different ways with an individual. For the purpose of this book, we will only discuss soul ties formed through fornication/adultery (sex outside of marriage).

A positive soul tie is formed between the marriage of a man and woman and is ordained by God. From the foundation of the world, God established the fundamental principle of what a Godly marriage is. In the confines of marriage; is where sexual intimacy is permitted and ordained by God (Marriage is to be held in honor among all [that is, regarded as something of great value], and the marriage bed undefiled [by immorality or by any sexual sin]; for God will judge the sexually immoral and adulterous). Negative soul ties are any bonds (ties) formed illegally (outside of God's law) and causes a defiling of the body, soul, and spirit. When a man and woman are intimate (sexually) they cling together and spiritually become one flesh as stated in Genesis 2:24, *"(For this reason a man shall leave his father and his mother, and shall be joined to his wife; and they shall become one flesh" (AMP).* There is something that happens supernaturally which cannot be understood from a fleshly perspective (carnal mind) when a man and women are intimate. When a husband and wife know each other intimately (sexual, emotional, intellectual, spiritual) they become one individual; one unit. In this same way becoming one can also represent a single entity.

As a consequence of having sex outside of the legal boundaries God established, I found my saved and sanctified self still having dreams of my ex-boyfriend. The dreams would include him getting saved and us possibly rekindling our love for each other. I would wake up confused because I had no desire on God's green earth to be with him. I found out in prayer through the Holy Spirit; the soul tie was not addressed.

The Holy Spirit gave me the tools and strategies to break this illegal soul tie once and for all. Listen, you must be willing to get real with God in order to receive a breakthrough in this area. Take this process very seriously and be sincere. This is a crucial piece to your total deliverance! This process is a personal step (between you and God) which will free you from the demonic grip and control soul ties brings.

You must **REPENT**!!! You must acknowledge you have sinned and failed to obey the principles of God! Biblical repentance always includes confessing your sin to God and then turning away from evil. Admitting your wrong and asking God to purify and cleanse your heart from the inside out cannot be overlooked. You must denounce all ungodly ties established under sin. Allowing the Holy Spirit to bring back to your remembrance any sexual and emotional soul ties formed outside of marriage is important. Be honest and open to the revelation. The Holy Spirit may bring up (bring to your remembrance) acquaintances you forgot about! You may come to the realization you've had more sexual encounters than you originally thought. Have the tissue box ready! God already knows everything and has already offered access to His forgiveness *(If we [freely] admit that we have sinned and confess our sins, He is faithful and just [true to His own nature and promises], and will forgive our sins and cleanse us continually from all unrighteousness [our wrongdoing, everything not in conformity with His will and purpose]) 1 John 1:9 AMP).* After confessing, repenting, and turning away from your sin, you will receive total forgiveness and freedom from your past. The enemy will try to bring up your past, but remember you are forgiven! You have been cleansed by the Blood of the Lamb!

Now that you have repented and received forgiveness through Jesus, there is one more thing left to do. You must get rid of anything associated with these ungodly soul ties (letters, cards, jewelry, furniture, clothes, etc.) In order to secure your freedom, you must be willing to utterly destroy any connection to the sin. You must do away with any legal access (of the enemy) to you through your gates (eyes and ears). Shut down phone conversations and social media ties. Give the enemy NO room to tempt you and stir up memories and old thoughts. I remember God had me collect every piece of jewelry and sell it. I didn't care how much it cost or how much the jeweler offered me. I wanted freedom! In order to embrace the new; you must be willing to give up the old! You must release in order to receive.

If you have children from a relationship, seek the direction of the Holy Spirit! He will give you the wisdom that's needed in this transition. You obviously can't get rid of your children, but you can start to cover, pray, bind and destroy any generational spirits of sexual perversion attached to your children through their bloodline. Set up boundaries of communication that are strictly related to the children until you feel you are completely free from temptations. Get an accountability partner who can be with you during conversations and drop-offs/pickups if you are not strong in this area. Remember you can do all things through Christ Jesus, who strengthens you!

Reflection

Take a moment and reflect. Ask the Holy Spirit to help you identify ungodly emotional, mental, sexual, spiritual; and abusive relationships. Write their names below. Remember your honesty in this is attached to your spiritual freedom. After completing your list; pray the prayer below. When the enemy tries to bring those individuals and your past up again, return to this page and remind yourself of this day! The day you were liberated, strengthened and forgiven!

_____

_____

_____

_____

_____

_____

_____

_____

Prayer to Denounce Soul Ties

God, You are wonderful and there is none like You in all the earth. You are Holy, Righteous and my Deliverer! I lean on You today God; trusting in Your process of healing and deliverance. I come before You Father, acknowledging I have sinned and falling short of the principles You established as it pertains to sexual intimacy. I have failed to walk in a way pleasing unto You. I repent of sinning against You and my body. I asked that You cleanse me in the name of Jesus. Father I ask You to forgive me and make me whole again. As I go through this process of purging and deliverance, strengthen me emotionally, physically and mentally in the name of Jesus. Wash me with Your Word and remove any residue associated with ungodly soul connections I formed with (Insert the name(s) of the individual(s) here). I denounce the act of fornication and adultery before You. I declare and decree I am no longer associated with these spirits and I am now walking in the spirit of Liberation! I declare I am forgiven and my sins have been cast into the sea of forgetfulness. I stand on Your promise that says if I confess my sins, You are faithful and just and will forgive us our sins and purify us from all unrighteousness in the name of Jesus. In the name of Jesus, I break every demonic promise and agreement I established with these individuals. Go to the heart of decisions Father and uproot and destroy every residue of hurt, pain and unforgiveness in the name of Jesus. I choose this day to forgive and walk in Your freedom and liberty. I submit and present my body to You Lord as a living sacrifice. Lead me and guide me into Godly associations and relationships in the name of Jesus. I declare I am no longer bound by my past, but I am moving forward in Your plans for my life in the name of Jesus, Amen!

Chapter 6

Preparation Tip 2:
Be Made Whole

Luke Chapter 8 records a woman who had suffered from a condition for over twelve years. She tried everything she could possibly do to get rid of this issue but was unsuccessful. She got word that Jesus was in town and made her way to Him. Forcing her way through the crowd with desperation; she touched the border of His garment and was healed immediately. Jesus says, "Who touched me?" His Disciples said it had to be someone from the multitude of people; it would be impossible to figure out. Jesus then goes on to say, "Somebody has touched Me for I perceive that virtue is gone out of Me." The woman fearfully comes forth and says, "I touched You and was healed immediately." Jesus says to her, "Daughter, be of good comfort: thy faith hath made thee whole; go in peace."

Being real with God can be emotionally painful (this was one of the hardest steps for me). After repenting and denouncing soul ties, you may feel saddened or discourage. You may have a deeper awareness of the issues (sin) you need healing of. Coming to the realization you had multiple sexual partners outside of His will, can be a tough pill to swallow. Remember you have escaped the chains of bandage and have been liberated, *"Therefore there is now no condemnation [no guilty verdict, no punishment] for those who are in Christ Jesus [who believe in Him as personal*

Lord and Savior]" (Romans 8:1 AMP) Even though you know you are forgiven by Him; now it's time to forgive yourself and receive healing physically, emotionally, and spiritually! Like the woman in the story above; you must be willing to press through the crowd (emotions, fear, and shame, embarrassment, self-unforgiveness) and touch the heart of Jesus through your faith to be made whole!

An important step in this preparation process includes you letting go of the resentment and anger you feel towards yourself! This may require addressing (getting to the heart of) the driving force (reason) behind some of the choices you've made. Be open to it. Did I rush into relationships because of something that happened in my childhood? Was it related to molestation, rape or abuse? Do I have issues with my dad not being around? Is it connected to low self-esteem and lack of self-worth? Whatever the source, GOD IS ABLE to heal you and make you whole again *"And the very God of peace sanctify you wholly; and I pray God your whole spirit and soul and body be preserved blameless unto the coming of our Lord Jesus Christ" (1 Thessalonians 5:23 KJV).*

Being made whole is the progression of being made or brought to a place of completeness; being made damage free. It's the original version of you. The "you" God created before the very foundations of the world was established. Being made whole includes spiritually, mentally, physically and emotionally. God is concerned about every aspect of our being. He never starts a work and not completes it. Scripture says in Philippians 6, *"I am convinced and confident of this very thing, that He who has begun a good work in you will [continue to] perfect and complete it until the day of Christ Jesus [the time of His return]."* Now isn't that really good news? He never leaves us or forsakes us. He is there with us every step of the way. Like a precise surgeon; the Holy Spirit will repair and mend every damaged area of the heart; going down to the very foundation of the pain.

In the process of being made whole; I discovered one of the main driving forces behind my poor decision making was hurt from my childhood. As an adult, I had the ability to say yes or no. No one forced me into anything, but subconsciously I was upset with my dad for being physically abusive to the family. I watched my mother and siblings along with myself get beat on a daily basis. I would hear my dad verbally, emotionally and physically tear down my mother. I would lay in bed and say, "I would never let a man treat me this way," So I would deliberately choose men with a bad reputation or a strong personality just to prove how strong I was. I had the idea that anything a man can do; I can do better. If he cheated on me with two women; then I'll show him how it's really done!

Never addressing the hurt and pain of my childhood kept me locked in a cage of despair and anger. It wasn't until I surrendered my life to Christ; the Holy Spirit began to show me the root cause of my hurt and the condition of my heart. In my 3rd year of being celibate, I remember on Father's Day, I was completely made whole and set free from the hurt of my past. I was singing songs to the Lord, and I heard the Holy Spirit say, "You must forgive your dad" I was thrown for a loop because I thought I had forgiven him. The Lord said, "There is still some residue Keisa. When he calls, why don't you answer the phone? When his name is brought up why do you still get upset?" The Lord was right. I started to cry, and I felt deliverance all over my body! The Lord gave me some instructions that day. After the completion of what He told me to do; there was this incredible agape love that filled my hurt for my dad. The anger was replaced with love! This happened supernaturally! I was made whole FOR REAL!

When we allow the complete work of healing to take place by the Holy Spirit; the sooner we will be in place to receive the promise (husband). Jesus's finished work on the cross gives us unrestricted access to true forgiveness, and we are MADE whole. In this place of wholeness, we are equipped and fitted for marriage/divine covenant. Today the Holy Spirit is asking, "Will you be made whole?" Let Him heal you from the inside out. Let the All-Sufficient God complete you!

Reflection

Allow the Holy Spirit to minister to your heart in this moment. What is He revealing to you? Is there a place in your heart where traces of residue have prevented you from receiving His complete deliverance?

_____

_____

_____

_____

_____

_____

_____

_____

_____

_____

_____

_____

_____

_____

_____

_____

Chapter 7

Preparation Tip 3:
Get Rid of the Fairytale Image

One morning I woke up from a dream of a wedding. In the dream, my husband found me and proposed in front of my entire family and friends. It was beautiful. When I came out of the dream, I lay in bed and allowed my imagination to go! What I saw in the dream was not good enough for me. Instead of immediately casting my imagination and thoughts down, "*Casting down imaginations, and every high thing that exalteth itself against the knowledge of God, and bringing into captivity every thought to the obedience of Christ*" *(2 Corinthians 10:5 KJV);* I choose to add a little more. I remember visualizing my husband whisking me off my feet and not having to worry about a thing! He bought me a new home, a car and we had lots of money. For the first time, I didn't have to think about bills. Mighty God Hallelujah, I thought to myself. He had so much money I didn't even need to work. My day included shopping, praying and then shopping some more. He was my knight in shining armor coming to rescue me from all my bills; I mean burdens lol. What a dream, right? Who wouldn't get excited about something so remarkable?

God is so amazingly patient. He will let you go only so far before He wheels you back in with the TRUTH. Scripture tells us the TRUTH is what makes us free. I remember the Holy Spirit saying, "What is that Keisa?" This question immediately got my attention. I answered, "Surely You know Lord." I continued by saying this is what it's going to be once I get married. It's so wonderfully beautiful I thought within myself. Then I remember hearing, "Who told you that? Who told you it would be this easy?" Now the Lord had my full and undivided attention. I received a strong rebuke. My imagined idea of marriage was nowhere near or slightly close to a Godly marriage. If I didn't get it before, I surely got it after this rebuke. He said there would hard and difficult times. There would be moments where our faith would be tested. There would be challenges along with victories. This was nothing like I imagined!

Fairytale ideas of marriage subconsciously get imprinted in our minds from the time we are born. From Disney movies to romance novels; we develop a picture of what society says a "perfect" relationship is. These unrealistic viewpoints form the way we think and interact with others. Marriage is not the answer to all our problems; the answer solely is found in Jesus. Until our minds have been washed and purged; we will never be in a position to handle the weight of a Godly Kingdom formed marriage. With unrealistic expectations; we will miss out on anything God has prepared.

One of the weapons to defeat the "fairytale syndrome" is to see what God says about love and marriage. Genesis 1:27-28 gives the foundational purpose of marriage *"So God created mankind in his own image, in the image of God he created them; male and female he created them. God blessed them and said to them, "Be fruitful and increase in number; fill the earth and subdue it. Rule over the fish in the sea and the birds in the sky and over every living creature that moves on the ground."* Our expectations for marriage should be formed by the word of God. He is the Architect, and we must follow the blueprint.

Secondly, we must stay away from marriage haters! Stay connected to Godly counsel and people who have been married for years. Some of the greatest wisdom and understanding of marriage I received was through conversations with Godly leaders in the Body of Christ. The wisdom they imparted is worth more than gold. They have been through the trenches and rose from the dirt by the grace of God and can share spiritual nuggets to deprogram your way of thinking SUCCESSFULLY!

Lastly, avoid watching movies or television shows that portray ungodly relationships. Again, if this gets down in our spirit, we will begin to form unrealistic expectations of marriage and relationship. This will absolutely cause us to make the wrong choice through compromise and find ourselves in a place of frustration.

Reflection

What are your thoughts on what a marriage is? What should it look like? Write it down. Now compare your perception of marriage to what the word of God says and what God has shared with you. Are they one in the same? If not, why?

_____

_____

_____

_____

_____

_____

_____

_____

_____

Chapter 8

Preparation Tip 4:
Get in the Word and Stay There

Sometimes we fail to really understand the power in and of the Word of God. The more Word we have, the more equipped we are to defeat the enemy. The Word of God is our weapon of mass destruction. It's the most valuable weapon in the arsenal of protection God has provided for His people. The Word is mentioned in the Armor of God in Ephesian 6: 8-10. It tells us to take on the Sword of the Spirit which is the word of God. Heaven and earth will pass away, but the WORD will never pass away.

If Jesus used the WORD, we are definitely not exempt! Matthew 4 records Him being lead into the wilderness by the Spirit to be tempted by the enemy. The tempter came to Him and said, "If you are the Son of God, tell these stones to become bread." Jesus responds, "It is written: 'Man shall not live on bread alone, but on every Word that comes from the mouth of God.' The enemy tried two more times to convince Jesus to submit. Each time Jesus gave Him the Word! Scripture goes on to say the enemy left Him. When we humble ourselves before God (submitting to His way), we can resist the devil, and he will flee! God has given us the same power and authority in His word to resist the enemy. He has provided the way of escape through His Word! The enemy only responds to the Word! In order to consistently defeat his tricks, plots, and schemes; we must speak the Word.

We will never experience victory in preserving our bodies; honoring our commitment to God without His Word. We are not fighting against flesh and blood! This is not a natural battle; guns and knives will not work. Earthy weapons will do us no good! We are engaged in a spiritual war with rulers, against the authorities, against the powers of this dark world and against the spiritual forces of evil in the heavenly realms. Only the Word of God gives us the Authority needed to command the enemy to flee. It is not in our power or understanding but through God's Word alone. Again, the enemy only responds to the Word of God! Using carnal weapons; we are defeated before we even get started. The less Word we have; the less prepared we are to overcome the temptation of the enemy.

Stay in the Word! I can't emphasize this enough! Every time I experienced the strongest temptation or desire to give in to fornication, can be traced to times I got out of the Word. The enemy is keeping watch! He knows exactly when to strike. Demonic forces are keeping a written record of our habits and how we respond to temptation and stimuli. This is all the more reason we cannot afford to slack off on the Word. Read the Word in the morning, in the afternoon and right before you go to bed. Let it play while you're sleeping; even when you're driving! We can never get too much Word.

If you are struggling with reading the Word, ask God to help you fall in love with His Word; asking God to give you a spirit of study. He will begin to open up the Scriptures before your eyes; revealing His secrets and thoughts.

Reflection

Take a moment to reflect. What are your go-to Scriptures when you are warring against your flesh? After reading this chapter, what has the Holy Spirit revealed to you? Write it down. When you are struggling; come back to this chapter and re-read what the Holy Spirit spoke to you in this moment.

_____

_____

_____

_____

_____

_____

_____

_____

_____

_____

_____

_____

_____

_____

_____

_____

_____

Chapter 9

Preparation Tip 5:
Pray Daily

Along with reading the Word; we must pray daily. Daily interaction with God is a must! In prayer, we are not only communicating with God, but He is also speaking to us. As we deliberately set aside quality time with Him; we are strengthened and built up. We should pray continuously without stopping (Luke 18:1). Prayer is a powerful tool and should not be overlooked. Scripture says in James 5:16, *"The heartfelt and persistent prayer of a righteous man (believer) can accomplish much when put into action and made effective by God—it is dynamic and can have tremendous power."*

Prayer has tremendous power and empowers the believer. Without prayer, we are disconnected from our Source. I can hear the older mothers of the church say, "Little prayer, little power; much prayer, much power." The more you pray, the more power you will receive from God to defeat the enemy. Through prayer, God will give you the tactics/plot of the enemy along with the strategies to defeat him. Prayer cannot be overlooked and must be seen just as necessary as the air we breathe.

Here are a few of the benefits I received through praying daily:
- Stronger Discernment
- Strategies
- Insight
- Understanding of my Purpose
- Directions and Instructions
- Deliverance
- Healing: Physically, Emotionally, Mentally and Spiritually
- Breakthrough in the Mind
- Cleansing of the Heart
- Divine Revelation and Wisdom
- Faith Strengthened
- Strength to Endure

What we receive in prayer can't be compared to anything. Prayer brings us closer to the Father. The closer we are to Him the more we desire to be pleasing to Him. The more we crave to be Holy and Righteous. There is no worse feeling than knowing you have disappointed God. In prayer, He shows you yourself in love and gives you the ability to be honest with Him. Prayer kept me connected to His heart! Prayer sustained me!

Prayer is one of the key areas in which the enemy will fight you strongly. He does not want you to pray! When it's time to pray you will notice the phone starts to ring off the hook; children demand your undivided attention; sleepiness overwhelms you, and it becomes difficult to keep your head up. Everything that can be a distraction appears when it's time to pray. These tactics are not new! The enemy wants you distracted by everything and anything just as long as you are not focused on Jesus!

In Matthew 26, Scripture records that Jesus went with his disciples to a place called Gethsemane to pray. He took Peter and the two sons of Zebedee along with him, and he began to be sorrowful and troubled. Scripture goes on to say that Jesus said to them, "My soul is overwhelmed with sorrow to the point of death. Stay here and keep watch with me." Going a little farther, Jesus fell with his face to the ground and prayed. He then returned to His disciples and found them sleeping. Jesus says, "Couldn't you men keep watch with me for one hour?" Then Jesus goes on to say something incredibly powerful, "Watch and pray so that you will not fall into temptation. The spirit is willing, but the flesh is weak." Since the flesh is weak, we must stay in His presence.

Watching, as well as praying, is the weapon needed to prevent you from falling into temptation. When you are weak; pray. When you feel lonely; pray! When you feel like having sex, you must pray so that you do not stumble and plunge back into the spirit of sexual perversion. Understand your adversary the devil wants to steal, kill and destroy your testimony! He is lurking and looking at all times to make a mockery of your testimony. The enemy is after your testimony!!! The way the devil seeks to destroy us is to get us to lose faith. You will lose faith and the ability to defeat the enemy if your eyes are off of God and onto the world. You must pray!

Reflection

James 5:16 says that the prayer of a righteous person is powerful and effective. How and when has prayer strengthened you in this process?

_____

_____

_____

_____

_____

_____

_____

_____

_____

_____

_____

_____

_____

_____

_____

_____

_____

_____

_____

Chapter 10

Preparation Tip 6
Date God

One Saturday morning I heard the Spirit of the Living God, tell me to get out of bed and get my nails done; prepare for a date. This may seem strange to some, but when you're in an intimate relationship with God, there is a constant flow of communication. You learn to hear and know His voice, so you act on it. I obeyed the instructions and went out to a restaurant. I struggled with understanding the purpose, but I trusted God had something important He wanted to show me. I arrived at the restaurant and asked for a table for one. After about 15 minutes I heard my name called, "Keisa party of two." I was slightly confused, so I started to speak up to say, "No I requested a table for one" but the Lord began to speak at that moment. He said there was no mistake; I was out with Him. As the waiter walked me to the table, I started to cry. I tried holding in the tears, but they began to flow down my face. I sat down at the table and heard the Lord say, "Order what you want it's on Me." After ordering my food, the Lord spoke to me in such a sweet soft voice. He reminded me of His plans for me and how much He loved me. He said He was proud of me for not compromising and settling. As you can imagine; the tears are flowing uncontrollably. I could not finish my food. It was as if I was falling in love with Him all over again.

Dating God just simply means spending quality time with Him. This includes providing an intimate space for Him outside of our hectic daily life. This is a divine set apart time for God to shower you with sweet loving words. While dating God, He shared I am a princess. I have shared this with many throughout the years. Some have responded with a confused look or maybe just didn't take me seriously. I was not moved by their faces or negative body language. Why? I knew what God said to me about me. There was nothing anyone else could say to make me change what I know I heard God say to me. During intimate times with Him, He would lift me up and strengthen me. He would wipe the tears from my eyes as I poured my heart out to Him. You too can experience this level of closeness and peace if you deliberately set time away with the King. Scripture tells us He is a rewarder to those who seek Him diligently. Seek Him; draw close, and He will share His secrets with you regarding your purpose in life. He will comfort you and strengthen you in your weakest times.

Reflection

Take a moment to reflect. How much quality time do you spend with God? Schedule a time to go out with God today. After your date, come back and record what happened. How did you feel? What did He say to you? When will you go with Him again?

_____

_____

_____

_____

_____

_____

_____

Keisa Jones

Chapter 11

Preparation Tip 7
Waiting with Expectation and Thanksgiving

After 10 years of waiting, I am now in a place where I am expecting and thanking God for all that transpired during this process. This is the very first time I feel I am ready to receive what God has prepared for me. It only took 10 years lol. I am excited about marriage but not consumed by the thought of it. I have finally aligned with the plan and purpose God has had for me all along. In this place, I am so grateful for the care and grace God has shown. I understand the only reason I can expect anything, including a husband, is because of His love and mercy! I was so broken and hurt, but NOW I'M HEALED! He has put me back together with his love. Yes, I am still waiting, but I am waiting as a whole woman. I am waiting patiently and not angrily. I am waiting with expectation and thanksgiving.

My prayer has changed from, "God, send my husband now!" to "Lord I thank You he will find me when its time." I find myself thanking God literally for everything that has happened. I understand that without it I would not be in this place. You can't be in a true position of Thanksgiving unless you expect it to manifest. Thanking God is something we do in advance because we know that it's already done. Scripture tells us in 1 Thessalonians 5:18, "*In everything give thanks: for this is the will of God in Christ Jesus concerning you"* (King James Version). I am thanking God for the Godly man of God after His own heart prepared for me. I am thanking God for the strength in my husband and the dedication he has towards the building of the Kingdom. I am thanking God for the strength to continue to wait. I am grateful for the model of a true man of God he will be for my children and grandchild. I am thanking God because my husband will love me like Christ loves the church. What a day it will be when he (the promise) finds me. My heart leaps with joy and waits with excitement.

During my 10-year journey, it was nothing but the Promises of God that kept me! I would read His Word (Bible) and also the things He would say to me while spending intimate time with Him. When I would read, re-read and read again, the things He promised me; it gave me the strength to keep persevering.

Reflection

I challenge you in these last blank pages to write out the things you are expecting and the things you have been grateful for along this process. I challenge you to write down the things God has promised you. When you are feeling lonely and disappointed, feeling like you are ready to comprise, throw in the towel; come back and read what you have written. Open this book and allow Him to speak to you. Let the words you have written remind you of the reasons why you wait!

_____

_____

_____

_____

Keisa Jones

Biography

Prophetess Keisa Jones is a passionate woman of great faith who has a heart to please the Father. She loves the Lord with every fiber of her being. She is an encourager, motivator and servant leader in the Body of Christ; being called as a Prophet to share the truth and love of God to the NATIONS. She understands the mandate from God to go to the nations and kingdoms to uproot and tear down, to destroy and overthrow, to build and to plant."

Keisa has served as an Evangelist, Intercessory Prayer Leader, Praise and Worship Leader, Leadership Support Member and Sunday School Teacher. She currently serves as a Minster and an Intercessory Prayer Leader Member among Open Door Worship Center, Carson CA. under the Prophetic Leadership of Bishop Deon and Prophetess Fannette Douglas. The Lord has given Keisa a heart and passion for Leaders and for those hurt and broken. She has dedicated her life to live as a true example of a BELIEVER and FOLLOWER of Jesus Christ. Her motto has become, **"For God I live and For God I die!"**

What's happened since I read the book:

_____

_____

_____

_____

_____

_____

_____

_____

_____

_____

_____

_____

_____

_____

_____

_____

_____

_____

Made in the USA
Middletown, DE
26 September 2021